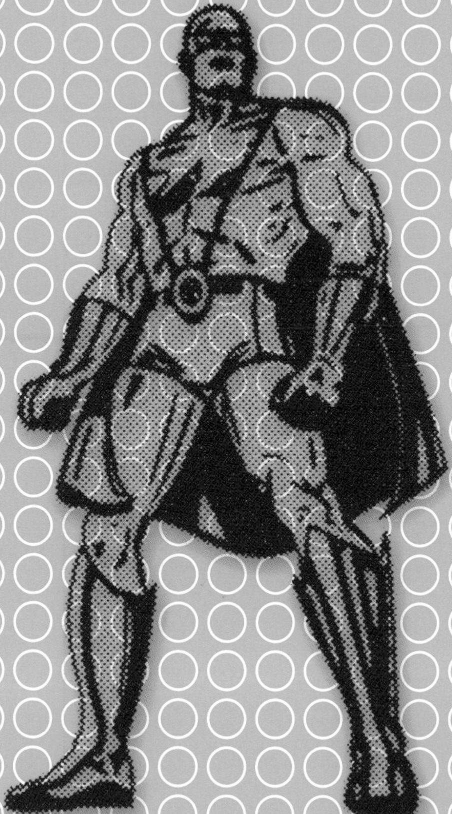

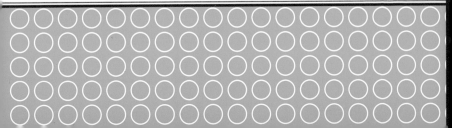

Publisher's Note

This book is for superheroes and their families. On no account should you attempt any of the intrepid feats and dangerous exploits shown inside. Do not follow any of the advice or believe any of the frankly implausible recommendations that are scattered with ill-considered regularity on every page. May we suggest instead that you go and have a nice sit down.

Published by Sterling Publishing Co., Inc.
387 Park Avenue South, New York, NY 10016

© 2005 by Gusto Company AS

Illustrations by Getty Images, Greg Paprocki and Tor Edvin Strom

Distributed in Canada by Sterling Publishing
c/o Canadian Manda Group, 165 Dufferin Street
Toronto, Ontario, Canada M6K 3H6

Distributed in Great Britain by Chrysalis Books
64 Brewery Road, London N7 9NT, England

Distributed in Australia by Capricorn Link (Australia) Pty. Ltd.
P.O. Box 704, Windsor, NSW 2756, Australia

Sterling ISBN 1-4027-2991-X

1 3 5 7 9 9 8 6 4 2

Manufactured in the United States of America

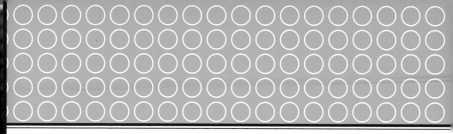

The Superhero Handbook

Michael Powell

Sterling Publishing
New York

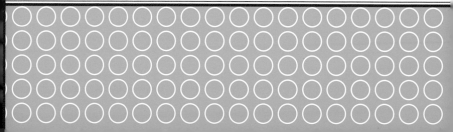

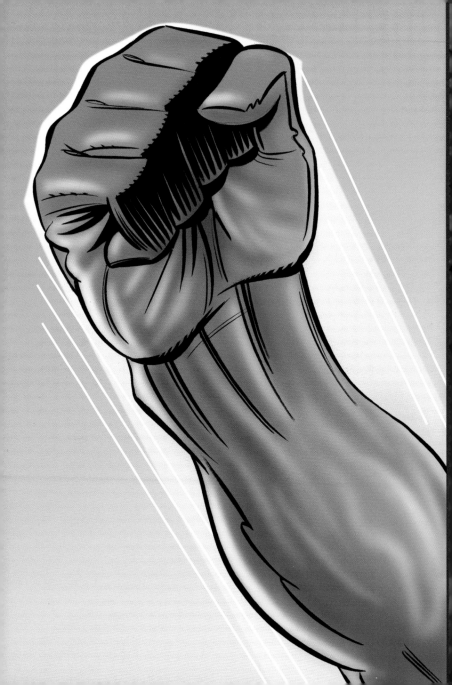

CONTENTS

CHAPTER FIVE
Superhero Boot Camp

CHAPTER SIX
Some Rain Must Fall

CHAPTER SEVEN
The Vegas Years

EPILOGUE

THE SUPERHERO HANDBOOK

Whether you are naturally amazing, have been sent here from a distant dying solar system, or just enjoy fooling around with radioactive slurry, the fact that you are browsing through this book suggests that you may already be experiencing subtle body changes that single you out from the rest of humanity. You'll have a whole heap of unanswered questions about your emerging superpowers:

Why do I have this overbearing desire to rid the world of evil?

What's this sticky stuff on my wrists?

Should I enter the priesthood?

Why am I so much stronger, faster, and more polite than the rest of my friends?

Why do I feel so washed out whenever someone hangs a large green crystal around my neck?

In this book you'll find the answers to all your questions, plus lots of advice on how to develop your superhero potential. You'll soon learn that you're not alone and that your retro hairstyling choices are perfectly normal (as well as your preoccupation with dubious rubber bodysuits). But you'll also discover that there's more to being a superhero than saving the planet, changing in phone booths, and struggling to disguise your fatal flaws.

You'll face important decisions such as whether to use your abilities for good or move over to the dark side (not forgetting, of course, that the good guy always wins); you'll experience highs and lows; you'll have the opportunity to travel the world, rescue innocent by-standers, and cheat death—and all this on a strictly voluntary basis.

What are you waiting for? It's time to embrace your destiny, set aside your selfish desires, and kick some butt.

CHAPTER ONE
Dreams of Destiny

Growing Up as a Nerd

As a counterpoint to your impressive superhero exploits, you will be a late developer. Your adolescence may be blighted by your being a bumbling goofball misfit loaner with some high-end eccentricities. Sound familiar?

Being a nerd is a vital ingredient in your superhero make up. It keeps your feet firmly on the ground, even when you are flying or rescuing kittens from burning buildings. Humans need superheroes to suffer their heartbreaks, reflect their anxieties, and share some of their weaknesses. So it pays to go all out, except in those unfortunate cases where your raw unharnessed superpowers lead to your being branded a freak and chased out of town by pitchfork-wielding neighbors. But neither do you want to end up as just another cleft-chinned überjock, the envy of those less well endowed.

What's the point of saving the world if it's too easy? Ordinary people appreciate only flawed superheroes, especially those who cultivate that "I've just slept in my clothes, because I fell asleep at my PC" look, and who never miss an opportunity to trip over furniture and spill the entire contents of their latte over themselves. In fact, a real supergeek rarely manages to drink any beverage without losing some of it either down themselves, a love interest, or someone in authority.

Pratfaller or Complete Klutz?

There is a subtle difference between pratfalling and being a complete klutz. Do your research. Most superheroes boast a DVD collection where the likes of Matt Damon and Laurence Fishburne are significantly underrepresented in favor of Charlie Chaplin and Buster Keaton.

When colliding with a door, tripping over a coffee table, or dropping a huge pile of documents all over the floor of your office just before an important presentation, it is paramount that you remain safe and controlled at all times and always maximize comic effect. For example, whenever you spill food or drink on someone, always compound your ineptitude by attempting to wipe it off with a tissue that is inadequately small, or spreads the stain even further.

Tick the boxes to discover your nerd quotient (NQ), and give yourself one point for each. You should aim to be able to check about half the boxes.

- [ ] Do you wear glasses?
- [ ] Are they broken and taped?
- [ ] Do you continually adjust them?
- [ ] Do you wear pens where other people can see them?
- [ ] Did you assemble your PC from scratch?
- [ ] Have you ever used a computer after 11:30 P.M.?
- [ ] Do you have more than two hobbies?
- [ ] Have you read all of Stephen King's books?
- [ ] Have you ever downloaded more than 20g from a binary newsgroup in one session (not including MP3s and porn)?
- [ ] Is your hair greasy?
- [ ] Can you understand the homages to other key sci-fi monoliths in the titles of *Star Trek* episodes?
- [ ] Is your shyness often mistaken for aloofness?
- [ ] Do you blush easily?
- [ ] Have you ever dissected anything?
- [ ] Do you have to concentrate when you are walking?
- [ ] Have you ever redesigned a household appliance?
- [ ] Do any of your T-shirts have writing on them (other than brand names and rock groups)?
- [ ] Have you spilled coffee on someone during the last month?
- [ ] Do you eat seeds?
- [ ] Have you ever played Dungeons & Dragons?
- [ ] Can you solve the Goldbach conjecture?

- [ ] → Does one beer make you fall asleep?
- [ ] → Do you know the difference between the words "substantive" and "substantial" (ignore if you are a politician)?
- [ ] → Have you ever corrected a teacher or professor?
- [ ] → Do you have biohazard signs on your bedroom walls?
- [ ] → Have you had a letter published in *Science News Weekly*?
- [ ] → Do you own a can of air (for cleaning electronic components)?

Always remember you tread a fine line between being endearingly gawky and just an irritating little creep who keeps breaking stuff, leaving a wake of expensive dry cleaning. Human beings are insecure, and will quickly cut dead anyone who is too different from them, be they superhero or loser.

Signs You May Be Special:
How to Recognize Your Powers

Superpowers take many different forms. Some supers reveal no outward signs of greatness, and only reveal their super side when they remove their glasses or their elbows start emitting cosmic energy. By contrast, others carry oh-so-unsubtle clues as to their real identity. (For example, Wolverine's ridiculous beastly muttonchops—what a giveaway. He might as well tattoo "Made in Pittsburgh" on his knuckles.)

However, many superpowers unfold gradually during adolescence. If this applies to you, this section may help you to recognize how you are different.

Superpowers often emerge in the most mundane situations. So here are ten of them and possible scenarios. However, don't jump to the wrong conclusion, as there may be a perfectly innocent explanation.

[1] You are making out with your girlfriend in her bedroom. She lets you go to second base for the first time. Just as you are unfastening her bra, you hear a cat call coming from the aquarium in the corner.

Superpower: You can communicate telepathically with marine life. Now might be a good time to tell the little voyeur to shove it.

Perfectly innocent explanation: Your Goth girlfriend keeps a pet wolf in a glass case in her bedroom and is training it to do tricks (whistling, contortion-ism, etc.).

[2] You are scratching your ear and have been trying to dislodge a stubborn piece of wax. As your irritation rises, so does the temperature inside your head.

Superpower: Your index fingers act as lasers.

Perfectly innocent explanation: You've been using your cell phone too much.

[3] You always get asked to leave the movie theater, planetarium, or pajama party.

Superpower: You glow in the dark.

Perfectly innocent explanation: You're a bigger nerd than you thought.

[4] Your dad is attempting to light the barbecue but it keeps going out. He goes into the garage to search for a bottle of liquid fuel. While he is away, you get a sudden urge to place two 16-ounce steaks on your head.

When you take them off, they are cooked medium rare.

Superpower: You are a walking ball of fire.

Perfectly innocent explanation: You are a real meathead. See a shrink and get your cholesterol checked, too.

[5] Whenever you miss the school bus, you still manage to arrive in class earlier than the time you left home.

Superpower: You can run faster than the speed of light.

Perfectly innocent explanation: You fell asleep at your desk again.

[6] Your unfinished homework spontaneously combusts on your way to school.

Superpower: You can conjure up hellfire as a weapon.

Perfectly innocent explanation: Your dog is on a diet, but has gotten hold of the cigarette lighter again.

[7] You can change channels on the TV just by thinking.

Superpower: You are Telly Kinetic (not to be confused with the more useful superpower of telekinesis).

Perfectly innocent explanation: You are sitting on the remote.

[8] You are walking in the mall with your pet tiger, when you are both transformed into super strong versions of yourselves.

Superpower: Looks like you've finally found a use for that Sword of Power.

Perfectly innocent explanation: There isn't one, dude. You are He-Man®.

[9] You are two years old. A truck falls on your father, and you lift it off him with ease and save his life.

Superpower: You have superhuman strength.

Perfectly innocent explanation: It is a toy truck.

[10] On a hot summer's day, whenever you leave your shades at home, everything in your field of vision appears to burst into flames.

Superpower: You harness the power of the sun to project an energy beam from your eyes.

Perfectly innocent explanation: You live in Florida.

Say Hello to Your Inner Superhero

It is to be expected that adjusting to your newly discovered powers may be an unsettling journey. You may abuse them for a while, until you learn to employ them for the general good. Well, who wouldn't use invisibility for a little innocent deviation?

Just in case you're tempted to abuse your powers or sneak over to the dark side, consider the downside of being a baddie:

[1] Staff training is an anathema. One mistake and you are obliged to feed the offender to your piranhas. Hence you are surrounded with incompetent idiots or seven-foot albino lumberheads who can't shoot straight. And you thought being a superhero was lonely.

[2] You have to live in a sewer or on a remote island, and your interior decoration is limited to brushed steel, marble, and black leather. You will also have difficulty selling your property, since few people want to live in a house disguised as a mountain.

[3] When you aren't busy thinking up evil plans to kidnap scientists who can invent a death ray for you, you'll be consumed with self-loathing and vengeful thoughts.

[4] Stupidity or pride will always prevent you from fulfilling your true potential.

[5] You will suffer terrible mood swings. One minute you're wringing your hands with glee and going "Bwa-hahahaha," and moments later you're stomping around in a frustrated rage. It's an emotional rollercoaster.

[6] You are restricted to two modes of self-expression: slow, measured speech or shouting.

[7] No one ever uses your real name.

[8] You get your toughest henchmen to beat up a good guy for an hour and a half and all they ever manage to do is give him a slight nosebleed.

CHAPTER ONE

[9] You end up doing all the entertaining. You invite people over to your lair and lay on unlimited martinis and Mozart while you explain your plans to rule the world, but do the good guys ever return the invitation?

[10] Crime isn't tax-deductible.

Advantages of Being a Goodie:

[1] You are more likely to get offered lucrative sponsorship and endorsement deals.

[2] You never have to say cheesy things like "Leave us" and "No, I expect you to die!"

[3] You get the satisfaction of rescuing friends and family from the evil clutches of your enemies, all the time. (Of course, if you weren't a superhero, they'd never be a target in the first place.)

[4] Goodies are generally taller, more attractive, and have better dental hygiene.

[5] Self-righteousness is a feeling that never turns stale.

[6] Your weapons are more reliable than those of baddies, which always seem to break down or run out of ammunition at a crucial moment.

[7] The loyalty of your colleagues is based on trust and respect, rather than fear or financial gain.

[8] You don't have the expense and inconvenience of maintaining exotic pets, such as a tank of sharks, pack of psychotic Dobermans, or an inscrutable long-haired cat (that requires regular grooming).

[9] You can share your plans for the weekend with someone without having to kill them afterwards.

[10] If you've taken a serious beating, all you have to do to recover from a concussion or a fractured skull is shake your head a few times and rub the back of your neck.

Breaking the News to Your Parents

Telling your parents you are a superhero is not an experience people take lightly—whether you are on the giving or the receiving end of this bombshell. There's never a right time or easy way to break the most difficult news they are likely to hear. For this reason, some superheroes choose to keep their identity secret from everyone.

Stereotypical Ideas

Parents still have very stereo-typical ideas about what it means to be a superhero. They often believe it is just a matter of time before their son wears his underwear over his pants, and makes ludicrous puns. The truth often lies very far from this.

Parents worry about their children leading a life of what they perceive as unstable and alien to their own experience. The life of a lonely latex-clad social misfit is what many parents imagine for their superhero child.

"Mom, Dad . . . I've got something to tell you."

If you are strongly inclined to reveal your true identity to your folks, be prepared for some unexpected reactions. Your parents may have been suspecting that you have been leading a double life and may be relieved to get everything out in the open (even if you do decide to wipe their memories the next day). Here are some common parental reactions:

[1] "Thank goodness. We thought you'd taken to popping steroids like your aunt in California."

[2] "In that case, come over here and help me open this jar of pickles."

[3] "We didn't work hard to put food on the table so that you can fly off at the first sign of trouble. We expect you to become a realtor, like your father."

[4] "You don't have to lie to us, dear. If you want to wear tights, that's fine with us. Now pass the salt, and let's hear no more about the matter."

[5] "Now that you know who you really are, can you please do something about that ugly old spaceship that brought you here when you were a baby; it's been cluttering up the barn for years."

[6] "So you have superpowers. Is that what's stopping you from tidying your bedroom?"

[7] "It's your life. Just don't make the same mistakes as us."

[8] "In my day we didn't have the same choices you young people have now."

[9] "That's fine, dear. Just be careful."

[10] "You're not going out dressed like that."

Ten Tips for Parents of Superhero Children

[1] Remember that this is still the child you know and love.

[2] They aren't doing this just to get away from your crappy little neighborhood and move to the big city. They could go to college or join the army to do that.

[3] You can't catch superpowers from your child. They aren't contagious (unless you're a family pet).

[4] Don't be surprised if the family pet starts wearing a mask or suddenly becomes sentient. Your child may require an animal comrade with superpowers to complement their own.

CHAPTER ONE

[5] Don't take advantage of their superpowers by increasing their chores or sending them on errands.

[6] Don't offer to design a costume. It will look dumb enough without your help. You may not agree with their choice of costume, but bite your tongue. And don't insist on taking a photograph of them in it, either—it compromises their identity and is also really embarrassing.

[7] Feel flattered that your child trusted you enough to tell you—albeit because you demanded an explanation immediately after they rescued you from Dr. Psycho's ectoplasmotron.

[8] Your child is not doing this to make you feel disempowered, even though they could crush your tiny head with one blow of their mighty fist.

[9] It might be time to accept that grounding is no longer an option.

[10] From now on, don't be upset if they don't phone you as regularly as before. They may just be tied up somewhere.

Remember that you want, above all else, for your child to be happy, to be indestructible, and to look great in a spandex bodysuit, not to lead a life of crime-fighting secrecy of which you form no part.

Parents, What Parents?

We've rightly spent time dealing with how to break the news to your folks, but the clearest sign that you are destined for superhero greatness is that they won't be on the scene at all. The absolute best head start you can hope for in your superhero career is to be an orphan. Research has shown that having one or more parents who have bit the big one is a definite advantage. In fact, it's almost a prerequisite.

There are many possible reasons for this. Certainly the apparent trauma of losing one's kin can spur many people on to achieve great things. But equally it may be the subsequent nurture of a gingham and apple-pie upbringing by quaint elderly relatives that lays the foundation for superhero stardom.

CHAPTER ONE

Another important factor is the overwhelming cloud of guilt that many supers carry around, the belief that that they were somehow responsible or could have prevented their parents' demise. For many superheroes, having visible underwear is a crude form of penance stemming from these Oedipal feelings of self-reproach.

Anger is another common reaction, especially in those cases where a super has traveled halfway across the universe expecting to be provided with wealthy foster parents in a trendy apartment in New York and a weekend retreat in The Hamptons. After a reality check, followed by a troubled childhood driving tractors and feeding chickens on a farm in Nebraska, it's not surprising that the first thing many supers do is to move to the city and start cruising the streets in a turbocharged supermobile.

If you're stuck with a pair of happy, healthy parents who show no signs of cashing in their chips you may have to resign yourself to being ordinary. On no account should you go out of your way to help them slip their cable, but if you do happen to witness their demise, you wouldn't be the first superhero to express their penitential vengeance via the medium of elastomeric polyurethane fiber.

Don't Give Up the Day Job

When between crime-fighting assignments, if you cannot live off the patents of your scientific inventions or you don't enjoy a significant inheritance, you'll need a job that covers the rent for your seedy downtown apartment, guarantees your anonymity, and has a health plan (crime fighting is the second most hazardous leisure activity, after bear wrestling).

Superheroes often choose low-status jobs such as pizza delivery boy or tabloid reporter, but in fact, it is better to choose a less respected occupation, where your absences won't be missed (such as real estate agent or congressman). This can be very useful when you are detained by your evil nemesis on a remote Pacific island and it takes you several days to escape.

Many superheroes have recently been lured to France, where the four-day week and flextime means that they can save the world and still maintain a reputation as a dependable corporate workhorse. With skillful time management, Euro-heroes can fulfill all their crime-fighting commitments during days off and weekends.

No one said that being a superhero was going to be easy. There's more to it than having low-carb abs and buns of steel. In the next chapter we examine your painful journey from newbie to neighborhood numero uno.

CHAPTER TWO
Denting the Sidewalk

*Falling Off Buildings and
Learning the Hard Way*

Should I Use a Mentor?

Superhero Code of Conduct

*Dealing with Your Superiority Complex
and Starting to Become Really Cool*

Falling Off Buildings and Learning the Hard Way

When Jor-El advised Superman® not to punish himself for his vanity, he was speaking in an era when superheroes were well trained and self-doubt was no more than a whistle stop on the fast track to becoming a secular messiah.

Today's superheroes just don't have the same opportunities to develop their skills away from public scrutiny. They are thrust into the professional superhero arena, where they are obliged to grow up quickly and make their mistakes in the spotlight. Gone are the days when a superhero could hightail it to an ice cave in the North Pole to spend twelve years boning up on the accumulated knowledge that spans the twenty-nine known galaxies. Even spending a few days practicing how to balance on one hand in the middle of a swamp now seems like a luxury from a bygone era.

The pressures caused by inadequate training are compounded by the fact that the physical demands placed on the modern superhero and the fitness levels required are much greater than they used to be. At the same time, the general public has become more sophisticated in their tastes. Many of the traditional superhero skills such as catching a helicopter as it plunges from the roof of a skyscraper, or repairing the San Andreas fault, are now considered either clichéd, or geologically implausible.

In short, you'd better learn the latest skills, on the job and fast. It could be time to find yourself a mentor.

Should I Use a Mentor?

Superheroes often use a mentor to help them develop and focus their powers. If you decide to go down this path, you should learn to recognize the tricks of their trade. Spotting a mentor is the first challenge. Do you find a mentor, or does a mentor find you?

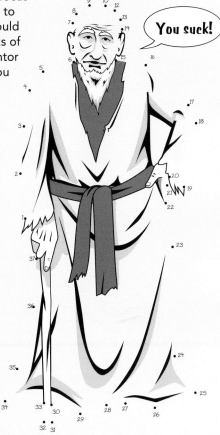

Can you find the mentor in this picture?

Mentors are always quirky and inscrutable, with hairy ears, and are usually considerably smaller and weedier-looking than you. In a room full of strangers, the most unfeasible looking specimen will always be the mentor. They will know your name and that you have been looking for them. They will also claim to have taught your father when he was your age. This is a cold-reading technique used by many mentors, to raise their status and make you believe they have mind-reading powers.

Study these three diagrams to see if you can spot which one is the mentor.

Answer: Open your mind. Any of them could be the one you seek.

Mentors, once identified, may state bluntly that they cannot help you, maybe because they have retired and are now concentrating on growing bonsai trees. Or they will blame you for being unprepared, saying something like, "I cannot teach you. You have no patience," or "I don't know if you're ready to learn what I have to teach you."

They will then invite you home for supper, after which they will thrust a paintbrush in your hand and shuffle off to run themselves a bubble bath without even telling you that the paint cans are in the shed. At this stage you may be dubious about their mentoring credentials, and begin to wonder what, if anything, they can teach you. Don't quit just yet.

The word "mentor" is derived from the phrase "mend door," because in order to learn patience, humility, and self-control, you will be expected to do a ridiculous amount of home maintenance. After three weeks of fence painting and wax-on/wax-off, you may suspect you are being exploited, but remember: mentors rarely accept payment for imparting their knowledge, and they almost always live in remote places where the nearest hardware store is over thirty light years away.

Don't expect any encouragement from your mentors, ever, unless you count a slight glint in their eye, or a barely perceptible nod when their back is turned. Superhero mentoring is the only teaching job in the world where the techniques of error-free learning and positive encouragement are thrown out of the window. They will remain inscrutably detached throughout. In fact, at the lowest point in your training they will almost certainly quit, claiming you're a failure and that you have been wasting their time.

Finally, just when you think you're getting the hang of it, they'll blindfold you and set you the ultimate challenge: servicing their central heating boiler. Your work will be expected to meet federal minimum standards of

operating efficiency. Be sure to check whether you are working on a vented low-pressure or an un-vented high-pressure system before you begin.

The only indication that you have finally earned their respect is if they give you one of their treasured belongings (which is rarely something really cool like a '59 Corvette—the best you can expect is a Purple Heart or some other worthless piece of crap). If you can't wait that long, ditch your mentor, and take off before your training is complete.

Five things a mentor is most likely to say:

[1] "I cannot teach you."

[2] "You are lazy."

[3] "You are wasting my time."

[4] "Your father was just like you."

[5] "Again!"

Five things a mentor is least likely to say:

[1] "Well done. You're trying really hard."

[2] "Let's skip training for today—I'll call for a pizza."

[3] "Oh, damn, that'll do—we all know that evil henchmen can't hit crap."

[4] "You've changed your hair, haven't you? Ooh, it really suits you."

[5] "Now it's my turn to lie on the floor so you can drop a large object on to my stomach."

Superhero Code of Conduct

During the golden age of crime fighting, a superhero's code of conduct was simple: to fight for good. Welcome to the twenty-first century! Fifty years ago it might have been acceptable to insult your enemies, chain smoke cigars, and use unreasonable force. Today, a superhero must show sensitivity for and respect towards others (even master criminals) at all times.

[1] Superheroes have a professional responsibly to serve the community, protect innocent bystanders, further the knowledge of science, and ensure the rights of all to liberty, equality, and justice.

[2] Superheroes will never allow personal feelings, animosities, or friendships to influence superhuman conduct, except for unresolved parental issues, and the persistent lure of the dark side.

[3] Superheroes accept that they work on a voluntary basis and therefore should not gain financially or in kind when engaging in superhero activities, nor claim any Social Security benefits as their alter ego.

[4] Superheroes must use reasonable force at all times, and only after discussion, negotiation, and mind tricks have been found to be inappropriate or ineffective. For example, a superhero should not launch an entire building at an assailant or swing a tank around his or her head and then throw it to the horizon, if a simple punch to the head or a bent turret will suffice.

[5] Superheroes do not engage in sexual harassment. Sexual harassment is sexual solicitation, physical advances, or verbal or nonverbal conduct that is

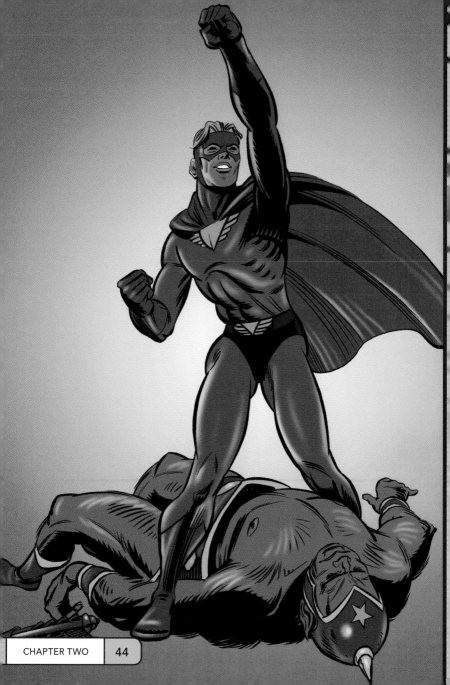

sexual in nature, that occurs in connection with the superhero's activities and that either is unwelcome, is offensive, or creates a hostile workplace or crime-fighting environment.

[6] When a conflict of interest arises during a crime-fighting assignment, superheroes should always follow the utilitarian premise that the best course of action creates the greatest good over the least pain.

[7] Superheroes always show up on time. Afterwards, they don't hang around basking in the praise and gratitude of the trainload of people whose lives they have just saved. They make their excuses and leave.

[8] Combative behavior should always be accompanied by a weak pun or one-liner. This helps to mitigate the aggression and shows that they indulge in controlled rather than gratuitous violence.

[9] Smoking a cigar while crime fighting is antisocial and damaging to the health of others. (If an archenemy can prove that he or she has inhaled a superhero's secondhand smoke, they may sue them for endangering their health, regardless of the fact that they were trying to decapitate the superhero at the time.)

[10] A crime fighter should not make any comments or engage in unfair discrimination based on age, gender, gender identity, race, ethnicity, culture, national origin, religion, sexual orientation, disability, socioeconomic status, or any basis proscribed by intergalactic law, even if an assailant is a fat, green, ugly one-legged transsexual Mekon.

Dealing with Your Superiority Complex and Starting to Become Really Cool

Someone once said that humility is a dish best served cold, or lukewarm . . . or something like that. The point is that it isn't, like, piping hot and really tasty and comforting, but something rather unpleasant. Maybe it should be a bit slimy too. Yes, that's better. Humility is a rather slimy dish that's best served cold. Like oysters.

Humility sort of gets caught in your throat, and you can feel it lodged in your windpipe if you don't take some water with it. No, that's not right. That makes it sound more like a dry cracker. What does humility taste like anyway? It is probably mildly astringent, with a minty aftertaste, so that once you've swallowed it your breath feels fresher.

Crap. It's revenge. Revenge is a dish best served cold.

Okay, so maybe we can say that humility is like a dry cracker after all. Yeah, the oyster analogy didn't feel right, anyway. So, where were we? Humility. As a superhero you'll want to look into that, because there's nothing worse than a cocky crime fighter with a superiority complex. Though who would blame you for thinking that you are a mighty figure worthy of worship? You would be forgiven for believing that you are more effective than currently popular deities who range from the utterly vengeful to the sort of laissez-faire divinities who never actually get off their celestial thrones to intervene in anything. Hence the presence of evil—which you spend every waking hour trying to conquer single-handedly.

CHAPTER TWO

Even on those days when you jump out of bed feeling utterly invincible, it is all too easy to feel that you are doing all this crime fighting on your own and that maybe the standard deities shouldn't be taking all the credit on the proactive righteousness front.

But being a god—a real paid-up, collect-money-to-repair-the-roof-heal-the-sick-light-candles-in-my-honor, kind of god—isn't all that it's cracked up to be. First of all, it isn't very cool. And the first thing that a superhero should be is cool. Proper deities limit their wardrobe to bed linen, which tends to restrict movement. They also eschew material stuff—which rules out all those gadgets.

Also, if you formed a religion, people would start writing hymns and oratorios in your honor, and it would be kind of hard to disappoint them by asking them to come up with something more funky.

So, get with the humility vibe and nip in the bud any aspirations to form an intergalactic religion. Besides, by now you'll be well on the way to mastering your powers and you'll be starting to look really cool.

CHAPTER TWO

CHAPTER THREE
You and Your Total Image

Creating Your Superhero Persona

In today's competitive superhero market, it is not enough to simply bend steel with your bare hands or construct objects out of mental energy—other people have to know that you have this ability. The choices you make about your appearance, your posture and body language, your voice and speech, the color of your tights, and the cut of your cape, convey powerful messages to others. This chapter examines your total image and how to make the signals that you send out work for you.

You are your most important asset. Superheroes with a poor self-image cannot make the sort of flawless and powerful impression that they want. A successful image is not about people admiring your anti-gravity boots or being dazzled by your new nemesis claw. It is about people noticing the real you, to the extent that once you have left the room they will remember that you looked professional and successful, even invincible, although they might not recall specific details about what you were wearing.

Here is a list of adjectives, some of which may describe you. Pick three that you feel are the most important qualities that you would like others to recognize in you.

Adamantine	Resourceful	Bulletproof	Tenacious	Untouchable
Invincible	Immortal	Supreme	Hypersonic	Unyielding
Powerful	Thaumaturgic	Theatrical	Perdurable	Mighty Accurate
Organized	Charming	Punctual	Breathtaking	Incredible
Reliable	Stalwart	Fearless	Imperishable	Awe-inspiring
Urbane	Polite	Indomitable	Amaranthine	Omnipotent
Creative	Cool	Dogged	Otherworldly	Supersonic

Next time you are saving the galaxy from a race of blob-like aliens that enter human orifices and consume their brains, ask yourself whether the three adjectives you have picked would be the same ones that your adversaries would use to describe you. How do you project these qualities in the few seconds before you shoot a bolt of electromagnetic energy into their gills to make their heads explode?

If you show pain, is there any chance that others will think you are invincible? If you bite your nails, will they really believe that you are otherworldly? If your voice is hesitant and you avoid eye contact, is it surprising that they see you as lacking in confidence rather than fearless or awe-inspiring?

Identify Your Niche and Establish Your Principles

Superheroes can be an introspective bunch. Whenever two or more muscle-bound freaks get together after-hours, once the drinks start flowing it isn't long before the topic of conversation shifts from protein milkshakes and advanced powerlifting techniques to a heated debate about the merits of the predominant Baconian meta-ethics of establishment law-enforcement versus the relatively undeveloped normative value system of emotivism.

Regrettably, most of the time, they just don't have the luxury of ethical dialectic of which they are so fond. So much of the job seems to be dominated by crisis management. Time and again superheroes report that they resort to the hit-first-defuse-the-bomb-think-later approach to crime fighting. When we have fifteen seconds to save the universe, most of us are so busy pummeling bad guys that lofty principles take a back seat.

For this reason it is vital to establish your principles and set your goals before you start your superhero career. Sit down with a pot of coffee and a pen and paper to identify the marketplace and the citizens you intend to benefit. Specify in detail the kind of superhero services you wish to provide. Before throwing a single punch, aim to have at your fingertips a detailed analysis of the criminal and innocent bystander demographic.

You may choose to focus solely on domestic issues, fighting on a single planet on behalf of the disenfranchised. Or, you may decide to protect the inhabitants of an entire galaxy, without making any judgment about their social status or moral integrity.

CHAPTER THREE

Armed with this preparation, you are more likely to avoid knee-jerk reactions to any crisis. A modern crime fighter should aspire to be a freethinking anti-establishment hero, arguing for morality in all its shades of gray, as opposed to just laying down the law. For example, most supers would agree that a silver-haired lady shoplifting tins of tuna chunks to take home to her litter of homeless strays is a less deserving candidate for judicial execution than a ski mask-clad bank robber or a corporate mogul falsifying the accounts of his poorly audited plasma energy empire. However, a die-hard handful of superheroes still insist on being zero-tolerance enforcers of morality, representing the law-'n'-order view of events. Fortunately they are a dying breed, since most of them, frustrated by ethical dilemmas, have hung up their capes to become TV evangelists.

It is true that some superheroes pursue several successful years of crime fighting fueled only by the adrenaline rush of witnessing their parents being slain in a street mugging, but usually it takes more than revenge or the desire to wage an intergalactic war against evil to sustain your enthusiasm and popularity.

Devise a Mission Statement

This should be targeted and focused. A vague superhero is a dangerous one. In the absence of a clear mandate, or domestic agenda, you'll end up being swayed by powerful neo-con cannibal humanoid rat beings. Before you can say "sovereign planet" you'll be launching fusion torpedoes at any solar system that you suspect is harboring your archenemies, rather than coming back to your primary duty, which is, of course, to externalize questions of duty and community and choose between prioritizing justice or promoting the sort of social inclusion that precludes an eighty-year-old animal lover from breaking the law.

Zero-tolerance approaches to morality often flounder because they fail to take account of the fact that all of us are a complex mixture of conflicting and competing desires. Is "ridding the world of evil" a realistic or even a desirable goal? It's a fine aspiration, but when you look at the reality of a universe without the naughty bits, it has greater repercussions than merely the loss of a corollary to all that is good.

What's the point of being bulletproof if there are no bullets? You wouldn't just be out of a job; you'd cease to exist. Action heroes are the sum of their actions. They rely on moral ambiguity for their identity in the same way that capitalism relies on the unequal distribution of wealth. Could that be why you can never quite bring yourself to dispatch your enemies decisively, and they always escape to fight another day? Besides, aren't crime problems generally far better addressed by social or economic policy than law-enforcers in tights?

CHAPTER THREE

The Three Ls–Leather, Latex, and Lycra: How to Choose and Make Your Costume

[1] Choose a fabric that is hardwearing, waterproof, flame-retardant, and won't show underarm sweat (e.g., light colors are best, whereas blues and reds stain easily).

[2] The fabric must allow freedom of movement, while at the same time showcasing your well-honed body to its full potential.

[3] The outfit should be machine washable and colorfast to 150 degrees Fahrenheit, otherwise you'll have a lot of explaining to do at the dry cleaners, or you'll have to run a cycle just to wash one garment.

[4] Decide whether to wear your superhero gear underneath your regular clothes (no need to carry around your outfit, but can get very hot) or change into them (fanny pack never leaves your side—what a drag).

[5] Decide whether to wear your undergarments on top or underneath your outfit.

[6] When in civilian clothing mode, choose a trademark prop to disguise your real appearance (e.g., pair of spectacles, comb-over, or permanently flared nostrils).

[7] Leather looks great on supers; suede does not, especially when it's fringed with tassels. It's wildly impractical and stains easily. As a general rule, don't use anything for your costume that you might find on a lampshade.

[8] Be scrupulous about your stitching; it's the first detail that your enemies will notice. Clothes make the crime fighter; can you think of even one naked superhero who has been a success?

[9] Don't get hung up on the whole cape thing. It's lame. 'Nuff said.

[10] Choose your sidekick's costume; if you're going to look dumb, then you want to make sure he looks even dumber.

Choosing a Strapline and a Catchphrase

Once you've chosen your costume, you'll need a strapline and catchphrase. Pick one of the four sentences below and use random words from each column to fill in the blanks:

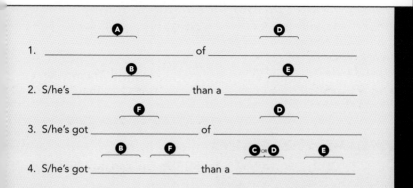

1. _____ **A** of _____ **D**

2. S/he's _____ **B** than a _____ **E**

3. S/he's got _____ **F** of _____ **D**

4. S/he's got _____ **B** **F** than a _____ **C** or **D** **E**

A	B	C	D	E	F
Bringer	better	clean	asbestos	bagel	arms
Crusader	crazier	crowded	blue	bomb	breasts
Defender	faster	dizzy	darkness	elephant	buns
Hero	hairier	exciting	fire	freight train	ears
Keeper	harder	exploding	freedom	hamburger	elbows
Killer	hotter	flavorsome	gold	horse	eyes
Leader	larger	gigantic	justice	monkey wrench	fingers
Man	longer	handsome	lead	NFL linebacker	hands
Protector	louder	insistent	pink	panther	internal organs
Rescuer	nicer	moist	plastic	pillow	knees
Slayer	sexier	mushy	smoke	ship	legs
Soldier	smarter	rabid	steel	speeding bullet	nostrils
Warrior	stiffer	sharp	stone	thunderstorm	shoulders
Watcher	taller	smooth	truth	volcano	thighs
Woman	tougher	solid	wood	weekend	wrists

Don't worry too much if you can't come up with a catchphrase now. But do pay attention to which sound bites you find yourself repeating, because a catchphrase is a surefire way to grab people's attention. You'll know you've left your inimitable mark on the public consciousness when a stranger points at you in the street, blurts out one of your lines, then doubles over in a medley of snorts and inane giggling.

Catchphrases You Shouldn't Use

Picking a catchphrase that is memorable, effective, and gets you taken seriously is harder than you think. Here are some that never quite made it:

[1] "I will return momentarily."

[2] "Don't make me angry, or I'll get a nosebleed. You wouldn't like me when I do that."

[3] "This looks like a job for . . . "

[4] "Up, up, and up a bit further."

[5] "Don't make me rip my pants!"

[6] "It's tickling time."

[7] "Trick or treat."

[8] "Leave nearly everything to me."

[9] "I am jurisprudence."

[10] "Turned out nice again."

Crafting an Alter Ego

Crafting your alter ego is crucial because it will determine how you fill your time between crime-fighting assignments. You want to choose a character that is boring enough that you don't attract attention, but not one who is so dull that other people feel like chewing their arms off when they are left alone with you.

For many supers, living within the confines of their alter ego can be a frustrating, and even boring experience. Sure, after a heavy bout of crime fighting, you may long to kick back with a bottle of beer or relax in a scented bath, but for many supers, being a civilian is about as interesting as the skin floating

on a bowl of clam chowder. They feel trapped in a kind of limbo, putting their lives on hold until the next galactic crisis.

Remember, if you stayed in your superhero character all the time, you would quickly burn out. From time to time you need to take the "u" out of "superhero" without feeling guilty because you aren't on the streets knuckle-whipping lowlifes. When we take more care of our alter egos, we actually become much more balanced and consequently more ready to call forth our most violent impulses and put on an awesome display of visual combat when it is required.

Many ordinary people fantasize about being a superhero; for men and women of steel, the opposite should be true. You should yearn for the mundane, relish the day-to-day humdrum of workaday living, and stop trying to be so perfect. To err is human. But who said that they should have the monopoly on erring? You have as much right as the next person to open the refrigerator and have a tub of overripe raspberries fall out and stain your new shirt. When you find a teaspoon in the sink moments after you've switched on the dishwasher, revel in your ability to make dumb mistakes. The next time you lose your car keys, blame the children. Don't allow your lightning-fast reactions, kinetic metal manipulation, or cosmic awareness to deprive you of a uniquely human experience.

The minutiae of alter-ego life can be just as interesting, unpredictable, and downright enjoyable as apocalyptic showdowns against the backdrop of a shattered inner-city wasteland. Have you ever pulled a door and then realized you should have pushed, even when it's clearly marked? No, of course you haven't, but you don't know what you're missing.

So enjoy your alter ego; it gives you a chance to dress up and be something which you aren't— one of the little people.

Accessorize: Hiring a Sidekick

Hiring a sidekick can be a key part of any superhero's image, but it is a major responsibility that should not be taken lightly. Once you take on a caped companion, you become an employer, with all the paperwork and responsibilities that go with it.

There are particular barriers to the engagement of sidekicks, not least the burden of ongoing training. Research shows that single-practitioner superheroes are often reluctant to get involved in sidekick training. This involves lots of sidekick time, traveling, and accommodation expenses. Many supers cannot afford to have one of their key workers absent. They may also lack the infrastructure to introduce and manage training initiatives, since so much of crime fighting is about facing new challenges and being prepared to improvise in the face of danger. An outward-bound course is a poor substitute for battling an army of flame-breathing, giant, tentacled jellyfish. Another real fear is that you spend time and effort to train sidekicks only to find them head-hunted by rival superheroes, or kidnapped and used as bait to lure you to the lair of your evil archnemesis. For these reasons many superheroes see sidekicks as nothing short of a liability and an administrative nightmare.

Help Wanted

Place a classified ad in the trade publications, by all means, but you may find that the best place to recruit is out on the streets.

When recruiting, it is important to avoid some common pitfalls. As an equal opportunities superhero, you must be prepared to consider sidekicks from all walks of life. This means you cannot discriminate on grounds of age, gender, or disability. Don't dismiss a sidekick just because they use a wheelchair. They may have telepathic abilities that far exceed your own. Always check sidekicks' references. However, sometimes they may have a legitimate reason for being unable to provide them, such as their last employer was recently eaten by a radiation-mutated praying mantis on the island of Zorgel.

Sidekicks must be shorter and younger than you and not be afraid to embrace the cross-dressing side of their personalities. However, sidekickery attracts lots of deviants who are only interested in the job because it indulges their desire to dress up in latex and leather.

They should also be great at coming up with one-liners, but know when to shut up. An over-talkative sidekick can quickly become an irritating distraction.

Some sidekicks will be overqualified for the job and have superpowers that may make you wonder why they aren't superheroes. Proceed with caution. If their answer to the question, "Where do you see yourself in five years time?" is "I want your job," hand them their coat.

It's a real challenge to find a sidekick who accepts that there is a glass ceiling and absolutely no chance of career progression. But at the same time, you want someone who is motivated and proactive. Some may be taking the job because it is local or because they hope it will fit around their children's schooling, without having any real passion for ridding the universe of amphibious dinosaurs.

Now that you have been groomed for superhero success, it is time to examine the logistics of setting up and running a crime-fighting outfit. In the next chapter we discuss some of the day-to-day practicalities of being a figure of redemption and salvation and leading a life dedicated to making our streets and homes safer places.

CHAPTER FOUR
Strategic Super-Doing

Making a Crime-Busting Business Plan
Crime-Fighting Trends
How to Pick Your Mode of Transportation
How to Find Your Superhero Lair
Going Solo Versus Being a League Player
Crime Fighting on a Budget

Making a Crime-Busting Business Plan

Many superheroes think that the only reason to develop a business plan is to convince their bank manager or venture capitalists to lend them the money to develop their subterranean helicopter launch pad, or fund research into top-secret weapons. This view is a little shortsighted, however. A well-developed plan will provide step-by-step instructions on how to translate your superpowers into a successfully actualized crime-busting service.

You may believe that it is just not productive or even possible to forecast your criminal apprehension rate accurately, and it can be hard to place a value on your performance. Many aspects of it will be non-quantifiable, such as the smile on an eight-year-old boy's face when you ruffle his hair and tell him to eat his greens, or the feel-good factor experienced by an entire neighborhood knowing that—thanks to you—the streets are a safer place.

Furthermore, how do you run a cost-benefit analysis on saving the universe? The choice seems obvious—the continuation of life as we know it, versus the complete annihilation of all carbon-based organisms within a given interstellar quadrant—the returns speak for themselves. However, just because someone is trying to destroy a solar system or exploit a wormhole in the space-time continuum does not mean that you should rush in with all fists blazing.

Believe it or not, you may already have pulled yourself back from the brink by employing a simple business plan, without realizing it. Perhaps you had been moonlighting as a bare-fist wrestler or in a circus sideshow before deciding that the demands for you as a superhero were sufficient to occupy your time and fulfill your destiny, without the need to exploit your superpowers elsewhere. This took conscious planning and decisive action.

CHAPTER FOUR

Business plans and feasibility studies give a whole-of-life-within-the-galaxy view of a crime-fighting mission before significant commitments are made in terms of your nanotech health levels or psionic energy expenditure. Your future as a superhero depends on you continuing to apprehend super-villains and thwart their evil plans. This means you cannot plan the future without some idea of how many demented schemes you will be expected to curtail, month by month, for the first year of your operations and beyond. What basis have you got for your crime-busting forecasts? Do you have hard evidence, backed up by statistical analysis, that your specialized skills and services will be up-to-date or in demand within the area of the galaxy where you plan to operate? In short, when there's a crisis and people say, "This is a job for ——" is it your name they think of first?

It is dangerous to assume that there will always be enough crazy scientists or morphing crab monsters to go around. You cannot guarantee that you will always be in the right place at the right time, or even that you will always be in favor (like every superhero before you, you will experience a period, however brief, when you are vilified by the press and lose the confidence of the public due to an unfortunate series of misunderstandings).

Even a popular superhero can go for months, or years, without a whiff of subterfuge. The superhero genre is massively oversubscribed. So rather than sitting at home waiting for the phone to light up, it pays to keep ahead of the game by calculating risk and setting targets.

Crime-Fighting Trends

Being a superhero has its peaks and valleys, and follows certain trends. While the formula may remain the same, the key ideas and paradigms that influence being a superhero today are not the same ones that will hold sway next season, and the one after that. Even the language that we use changes dramatically over time. This is never made more evident that on those embarrassing occasions when one hears a modern superhero trotting out the tired slogans of a bygone generation. For instance, any super uttering the words, "All in a day's work, ma'am" would be considered quaint and out-of-touch.

Crime fighting is cyclical and, to a certain extent, quite predictable. Every few years another crazy scientist hatches a plot to destroy the universe and the whole superhero industry starts to buzz with the anticipation that an event of apocalyptic proportions is about to kick off. Maybe a wealthy businessman has begun buying up thousands of planets with terraforming development potential. Rumors circulate that he is planning to cause a supernova on the western star board that will render large sections of the galaxy uninhabitable, and make his property rocket in value. Superheroes everywhere maneuver for position with a view to being called into action when the fireworks start. If you are unaware that something big is about to go down, you may be at completely the wrong point on your own business cycle. You may have just laid off your sidekick or reduced your stockpile of dilithium rockets when other superheroes are up to speed and preparing for major growth.

Being aware of the trends not only reduces your chances of missing big contracts, it also teaches you to embrace change and convert it into dynamic practice by showing that you should never take anything for granted. For example, were you aware that:

[1] Recent developments in planetary force field technology may soon render many of the conventional cosmic death rays of crazed power-obsessed evil scientists obsolete?

[2] Many criminals have downsized their operations to survive in today's competitive global crime market and find that they are able to dispatch their enemies or incompetent employees with a single breeding pair of well-trained piranhas, rather than an aquarium of sharks?

[3] Following the privatization and fragmentation of many train services and the corresponding reduction in punctuality, many bad guys are reluctant to tie people to railways lines?

[4] Many archenemies no longer bother with the formality of explaining their wicked plot in minute detail to a tied up superhero? (They simply send an e-mail.)

The way you react to a crisis should extend across your entire organization. Many crime-busting opportunities are missed simply because someone in your headquarters answers the emergency phone in a negative and unconstructive manner. Train everyone from the cleaning lady to the butler to take an interest in the caller. Even if you are unable to meet the requirements (for example, the crisis demands body duplication skills, which you are unable to provide), then creating a positive impression means they may still call you with a more suitable assignment.

How to Pick Your Mode of Transportation

There are seven categories of superhero travel: supermobile, animal, helicopter, motorcycle, flying, running very fast, and taking huge leaps. There is also teleportation, which renders all the others obsolete, but you can't always guarantee being on a planet that has compatible teleporting software. Until an industry standard is applied, it will always be susceptible to crashes of the most disastrous kind.

Supermobile

When you think of a supermobile, which one springs to mind? You too, huh? Can't get past the image of that black shiny retrofitted 1955 Lincoln Futura? See, that's the problem. We just can't get it out of our minds. Picture the scene: you're driving around in your supermobile. You get a flat and absentmindedly reach for the automatic tire repair button. But that's strange—you could have sworn that your sidekick wasn't wearing green tights . . . uh oh . . . "perilous paradigm shifts" . . . it looks like you're starring in your very own crossover fanfic. Let's hope that when you wake up from that nightmare you'll look into other methods of transport.

Animal

Have you ever fed a horse? Nothing licks the feeling of those horsy lips snaffling up juicy grass from your outstretched palm. Yep, an animal companion is a rare blessing. Loyal, strong, and ideal for getting from A to B, with the added bonus that when you're stranded in a frozen wasteland you can snuggle up to it to keep warm.

Helicopter

The guy that thought up the idea of putting a little rubber on the end of a pencil—now that was a good invention. Pity the same can't be said about the helicopter. It isn't that flying one of these babies is dangerous—crashing is the dangerous part. But if you opt for a helicopter, you'd better be ready to do a lot of crashing. Try to think of a film where the helicopter stayed in the air!

Motorcycle

This is by far the coolest way to travel. It has long been associated with crazy quests and classic scrapes with the law, which is why it makes the ultimate post-modern statement when driven by a super-do-gooder like you. Nothing beats the feeling of a pair of designer shades between your ears, a 2000cc engine between your legs, and the open road. Oh, and a pumpaction laser cannon, which you cock and shoot with one hand as you drive the wrong way down the freeway. Bitchin'.

Flying

It has been estimated that at any given time there are hundreds of thousands of people airborne. But only a handful of those will be doing it without the help of a jet engine. Whether you use web-based propulsion or your own airborne power, flying is an impressive and environmentally friendly alternative to airline travel. And if you hold your breath while you are flying, you won't create any carbon dioxide emissions.

Running Very Fast

This is a convenient solution, but it doesn't actually look as cool as you might think—outrunning a train makes you look stupid if your legs are running faster than the rate at which you are covering ground.

Taking Huge Leaps

Well, this one pretty much speaks for itself. Basically it involves taking one huge leap, then following it up with another one, more or less like the first, and so on. It's totally useless in stealth operations because you'll leave large potholes and micro-quakes wherever you go, but it's an excellent standby when you're angry and you need to get somewhere fast.

How to Find Your Superhero Lair

Many superheroes begin small, working out of their bedroom. That's fine—there's nothing wrong with that. You have to start a crime-busting empire somewhere. The problems arise when your business starts to grow. Many supers make the mistake of thinking they can hold on for a few more months in cramped living quarters—closet overflowing with capes and masks, positron converters under the bed, your first-edition copy of *The Necromonicon* languishing under a partially eaten slice of cheese on toast. Usually it takes a silly mistake such as knocking a week-old cup of coffee onto your only clean pair of tights, or mislaying your space boomerang for the tenth time in a week, to send you off to the corner shop to thumb through the real estate pages of the local newspaper.

There are many advantages to having your own secret lair:
[1] You can charge up the disintegration beam whenever you like, without miscalculating the combined gigawattage of all the appliances in the house and blowing the fuses for the whole street. You can even switch on the multi-dimensional transmogrifier without worrying whether your parents are watching TV downstairs in front of a raging electric fire.

[2] No more lining up to use the bathroom or the radioactive decontamination shower.

[3] You can come home at 2 A.M. after an evening of battling stone giants and fix yourself a snack without worrying about waking anyone up.

[4] You can stroll around in your underpants without having to slip anything on underneath them.

[5] Never again will you bring back a miscreant with plans for an evening of noisy interrogation, only to find that your mom needs the lounge for one of her bridge nights.

Whether you are in the market for an ancestral castle or a super-modern subterranean warehouse, choosing the ideal location is important. Your lair must cater to all your superhero needs, but you shouldn't neglect the home comforts. It is easy to be impressed by the large number of electrical sockets or by the handy subway station next door, and forget to ensure that you have adequate closet space or that your enemy interrogation chamber has under-floor heating.

Checklist for Buying a Superhero Lair

There are lots of factors to take into account when buying a lair:

Location

Choose a pad in the seediest and most rundown part of town. Sure, it's tempting to choose a picture box dwelling in a nice suburban crime-free area, but the long commute to hot spots of unlawful activity will soon become irksome, especially during the summer months. As a rule of thumb, if the view from your bedroom window is the fire escape of the neighboring property, you're in the right district. If there aren't at least three large household appliances smoldering in the street, you've gone too upmarket.

Space

Inner city living makes space a premium, but be smart and try to get as much storage as your buck will buy. Even the smallest cyclotron accelerator can fill a spare bedroom. In the old days superheroes shared their living quarters with bulky mainframe computers and reel-to-reel storage systems. Be thankful at least that the micro revolution has made it possible to achieve that hi-tech lair look at a fraction of the cost and space of decades ago, leaving you more money and room to house your ever-growing collection of antique grappling hooks.

Impregnability

This seems self-evident, but you'd be surprised how many supers settle for cheap cavity walls and flimsy stud partitions, rather than the minimum recommended level of protection, which is a forty-foot thickness of steel-reinforced granite. This will significantly reduce your living space, but when the inevitable location breach occurs, you'll be glad you tolerated a kitchen the size of a telephone booth in favor of home security.

Read the Lease

If you are a leaseholder, it is imperative that you check the lease, as it may have a clause prohibiting you from using the property as a base of operations for a crime-fighting empire. Or else, it may grant this use under restrictive conditions such as forbidding the storing of radioactive isotopes, or conducting research into ways of mutating human DNA.

Resale Value

In addition to your preferences and requirements, you should also be mindful of what others might like. The less unique superhero characteristics and the more commonly desired features your lair has, the wider its appeal and the higher the price you'll get when you sell. Just because you can't imagine life without a breakfast bar that flips over into an operational hub doesn't mean that others will, no matter how many blinking lights and analog switches it has. You may want a helicopter pad, for example, but they generally take away from the resale value. By contrast, off-street parking can add thousands.

Going Solo Versus Being a League Player

The first decision you need to make before you start is about the organizational structure. Do you want to be a sole proprietor, a partnership, or a crime-fighting corporation? This depends on several factors:

[1] The degree of control you want over delivering justice. Are you happy to delegate routine tasks such as vigorous punching and kicking to other individuals, or a team? Also, are you willing to share resources, such as a butler, heli-pad, and interwave transducer?

[2] The need to protect yourself from personal liability (e.g., what do you do when you have to drop the old lady because you're saving the cable car full of children?).

[3] The ability to attract criminal types. A league of superheroes is a bigger challenge than one lone super.

[4] Tax considerations: if your turnover of shady types exceeds a certain level, there are sound logistical and financial incentives for being part of a corporation or league.

The main reason that Earth-based superheroes form leagues is to fight off the threats from outer space. Terrestrial crises can be dealt with by individual supers working on their own, but when you want to protect a single planet from attacks from outer space, you really need to team up with other superheroes. This is historically the way that justice leagues have evolved in the past.

When a giant starfish with atom-bomb absorbing, mind-stealing, and mind-control powers pays Earth a visit, or a would-be sorcerer summons ancient demon-like entities, the one-man show must not go on, especially if it coincides with a large and dangerous meteor shower heading the same way. Sometimes you just have to make time for yourself and accept help from others. Besides, you will find there are occasions when you just can't be bothered to change your clothes, let alone fly off for an evening of battling evil. That's when having super buddies can be a big advantage.

Start off with three colleagues with a variety of complementary skills, maybe one who can fly, a water-based entity, and a robot/alien. The downside of superhero leagues is that they can grow out of hand. Seven seems to be the optimum number. Soon you have to move your base from under a mountain to a satellite headquarters in geosynchronous orbit, and then decamp again to a watchtower on the moon. Again this progressive migration to larger quarters in outer space makes sense, but plays havoc with your credit rating.

Make sure that there is no overlap between your skills and those of the other superheroes in the team. This avoids the embarrassment of a situation where you yell "my call" only to find that another super has sprung into action, or, worse, you both do a shoddy job, thinking someone else will pick up the slack. However, you must also be prepared to be played in a position that doesn't suit you, to benefit the team, and also, it can get a bit boring executing the same plays all season. But a team needs a consistent strategy, which means you can't be as impulsive as when you were a solo prima donna.

However, when superhero leagues split, they split badly, usually because one member wants to resume a solo career. The rift caused by the frustrated aspirations of the other members of the league can take years to heal.

Crime Fighting on a Budget

Occasional crime fighting and being a tightwad need not be mutually exclusive. Whatever kind of income plan you have there are numerous ways to minimize expenditure and still work wonders.

[1] Buy in bulk. Check out the buy-one-get-one-free offers at your local artillery outlet. Always make a list of essential items so you won't be tempted to buy on impulse. Choose generic ammunition rather than being seduced by designer brands (your archenemy certainly won't make the distinction).

[2] Manufacture your own munitions: make sure your kitchen cupboards are well stocked with staples such as potassium nitrate, charcoal, and sulfur, then buy ingredients tailored to your firepower requirements. Popular all-year-round choices include clover leaves, holy water, silver shavings, and white oak.

[3] Create a monthly budget and stick to it, even if it means coping without cigars and implosion grenades for a few days before pay day.

[4] Check your phone bill to see if you have optional calling features or additional services that you don't need. Put a bar on or buy a pre-paid phone card for interplanetary calls.

[5] After you have been exposed to a high dose of radiation and your skin is beginning to peel, don't waste money on expensive anti-blister creams. Apply raw honey for a naturally soothing and cheap alternative.

[6] Run your particle accelerator and other high-energy devices during off-peak hours, when electricity is cheaper. Call your utility provider for information about cost-saving tips.

CHAPTER FIVE
Superhero Boot Camp

How to Break Through Walls

How to Take a Punch

Leap a Building in a Single Bound

How to Defuse a Bomb

Swinging a Tank

Breaking Adamantine Bonds

How to Stop a Runaway Train

Vehicular Pursuit

*How to Save the World During
Your Lunch Break*

How to Break Through Walls

Punching through a wall with your fists is easy. For many supers it's a rite of passage, a defining moment that gives them an early inkling they may be special. Smashing your mitts through three feet of masonry requires extensive knowledge of structural mechanics, architecture, and planning law. So, always follow these simple safety precautions.

[1] Check that you are not destroying a load-bearing wall. Feckless removal of bearing walls causes cracking of finishes, sagging ceilings, bowed doors and window frames, or even the collapse of the building. If you are planning to throw the building at your enemy, then this is irrelevant, but if you want it to remain intact, you should calculate how much load is going into the wall. Then add new beams or columns to support the wall or enclose a new support beam within the ceiling before hammering lumps out of it with your fists. Having a sidekick with a structural engineering background can be a big advantage.

[2] Familiarize yourself with local planning laws. For example, in France, Spain, and Italy, you should knock down a wall only after checking with the mayor, who must rubberstamp any plans you have to alter the fabric of the building. Bureaucracy in these countries is notorious, so make sure you file a planning request at least three months in advance.

[3] If the property has listed status, or is a site of special historical significance, climb out of the window, or use the door, like everybody else.

[4] Use your X-ray vision to ensure that there isn't another superhero on the other side of the wall trying to break it down at the exact same time as you.

CHAPTER FIVE

How to Take a Punch

When you are punched by an ordinary person, it is important that you stand with your hand on your hips and remain implacable. If you register no reaction the person delivering the punch will stare comically at his hand in surprise. As he starts to back away, his friend will attempt to hit you from behind with a pool cue or a chair. That is your signal to pick one of them up with one hand and throw them across the room. If you are in a bar aim for the mirrors behind the counter; if you are in a bar where country music is playing, everyone in the place will start fighting each other.

When a big mean-looking thug punches you, catch his fist in your palm and then squeeze his fingers. He will then fall to his knees in pain, rather than attempt to kick you or punch with his other hand.

Whenever you are overpowered and are worked over by a bunch of evil henchmen, the only visible sign of injury will be a slight trickle of blood from the corner of your mouth. After the confrontation, wipe this blood away with the back of your hand and stare at it, then touch your jaw while moving it from side to side. Heroes always do this, though no one knows why.

Any injuries sustained during a fight will give you minimal pain until the moment when a woman attempts to clean the wounds, making you wince with pain, even though you have just taken a severe beating with virtual impunity.

Leap a Building in a Single Bound

Have you considered that leaping a building in a single bound is a less efficient use of your energy and takes more time than jogging around the block?

Were you off sick from school the day they taught you about work-energy theorem? Here's a diagram of the Sears Tower.

Suppose you were standing at A and decide to jump over it and land at B. It is 110 stories and 1,450 feet high. Traveling over the building and back down to the ground you would cover a distance of over half a mile. If you jogged around the block you'd only have to go a couple hundred yards. The airborne route is about four times the distance. If you want to do it in the same time then the

g-forces on your body will be . . . er . . . much greater, which isn't good if you're rescuing someone in your arms.

Also, the amount of energy required is enormous. Actually, we don't know how to work it out either, but we reckon that the force required to propel you over the building = your weight (say 220 lbs) x earth's gravity, plus some other stuff. So, basically, you've got to use lots of energy. Plus, all of it will be going through your feet into the ground, so even if you are careful to avoid making a crater when you land, you'll find it hard not to make one when you take off, especially if you lead with one foot.

In short, don't be a show-off. Wherever possible, run around a building rather than jump over it.

How to Defuse a Bomb

Once you understand how evil geniuses plant bombs and how they operate, defusing them or staying safe when they explode is routine:

[1] The bomb will usually be on a timer mechanism with a convenient LED display that tells you how many minutes you have left before detonation.

[2] All wires have different colors, so that you can decide which one to cut. It doesn't matter which wire you cut (red or blue), so long as you briefly place your wire cutters around one, then change your mind and decisively cut the other.

[3] Bombs rarely detonate at zero. There is usually a silence lasting three beats to allow any cameras present to pan back to a long shot of the building that is about to explode.

[4] In the case of old-fashioned bombs, the fuse will inexplicably burn for hours. This will give you ample time to rescue the damsel in distress and extinguish the fuse with an inexplicably handily-located water bucket.

[5] One bomb will always cause multiple explosions.

Swinging a Tank

With feats of strength, less is often more. A tank weighs between forty and sixty tons, whereas the Sears Tower weighs in at a massive 222,500 tons, the equivalent of about 4,000 tanks. Absurd as it may seem, throwing a building generates less of a wow factor than crisply dispatching a military vehicle. But the public will always have a soft spot for a superhero who can pick one up, spin it around his head a few times, and throw it the length of ten football fields.

The reason is this: Even cleaning your teeth is a symbolic act.

A tank is the ultimate symbol of impregnability and also of steam-rolling barbarism, whereas a building is a static lump of steel and stone.

So, never forget that the symbolism of your actions is more important than displays of brute force. For example, bending the turret back so that it points at the young rookie gun operator is a thrilling example of contained might, of symbolically turning the aggression of the aggressor back on himself. Wow, makes you stroke your chin, doesn't it?

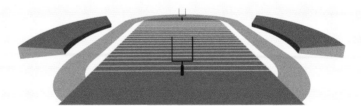

CHAPTER FIVE

Breaking Adamantine Bonds

When you are restrained in seemingly impregnable bonds, resort to passive-aggressive behavior, including sulking and sarcasm. Try to personalize criticism: an insult or casual remark from your captor will give you that extra resolve to break free of your confinement.

If you are tied up with rope, your captors will either botch the job, allowing you to wriggle free, or else you can guarantee that there will be a sharp object somewhere in the vicinity which you can use to hack through it or rub against until the rope frays enough for you to snap it. Failing this, there will be a candle or other means of burning through the fibers. However, bear in mind that you will usually have to maintain a conversation with one of your unobservant captors while you are doing it.

If you are gagged, it is customary to show resistance by shaking your head and making futile "mm mmm mmm" sounds for several seconds after the duct tape has been firmly applied to the lower part of your face.

After you have escaped from either rope or handcuffs, always rub your wrists a little to indicate that they were a bit uncomfortable.

How to Stop a Runaway Train

Using your bare hands to stop a train is always unnecessary. To stop an electric train all you have to do is disconnect the power and it will then decelerate gradually of its own accord. Do this simply by shorting the rails. Even a large diesel train does not drive the wheels directly; the diesel drives a generator which makes electricity, which is then transferred to storage batteries underneath the train. It is these batteries that run electric motors to drive the wheels. Simply disconnect the terminals to stop the train.

If you insist on flexing your muscles, bring the train to a gradual halt. If a train traveling at 250 miles per hour is stopped dead, the passengers will continue to travel at that speed (that is double their terminal velocity). In other words, unless you stop the train slowly, they will have more chance of surviving if you had dropped them out of an airplane without a parachute. A safe stopping distance is several miles.

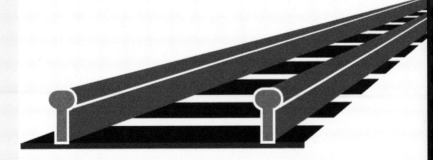

CHAPTER FIVE

Vehicular Pursuit

You may be driving a super-mobile, but you should always follow these ten simple rules:

[1] During the chase you will encounter the following: a fruit cart, a group of school children at a crosswalk, nuns, two men carrying a large sheet of glass, and a woman pushing a baby carriage (if you hit the carriage, it will be full of empty soda cans because the woman is a vagrant).

[2] The pursuit will always take you through Chinatown, a street carnival, a concrete drainage canal, or down a flight of steps.

[3] Pedestrians will always jump out of your way, even if you are driving on the sidewalk and approach them from behind.

[4] Any car that is being shot at will receive hits in the gas tank or windscreen, whereupon it will explode if it is being driven by bad guys; otherwise it will have no effect.

[5] It is possible to jump out of a vehicle traveling at high speed without sustaining an injury so long as you roll safely into a pile of refuse.

[6] After a long chase, if a bad guy crashes because of a basic driver error, he will take his hands off the steering wheel and cover his eyes with his arms before impact.

[7] Chases often end because the road hasn't been finished. Just before you crash through the barrier marked "Stop Danger," a road worker will attempt to block your progress by waving his arms before jumping out of the way.

[8] All cars can survive the most jarring landings after being airborne without any undercarriage modifications, heavy duty crossmembers, or beefed up torsion bars.

[9] If you hit a parked car, it will send your vehicle high into the air, but the parked car will remain rooted to the spot.

[10] If someone is following you, they will only start to drive erratically moments after you spot them in your rearview mirror.

How to Save the World During Your Lunch Break

We have already discussed in Chapter One the importance of finding a day job that gives you the flexibility to fight crime. One way we suggested you can juggle a mindless and repetitive menial employment with your heroic commitments is to fight crime on weekends and during contractual breaks, the longest of which is, of course, the lunch break. Most employers allow an hour for lunch, which gives you enough time to buy some sandwiches, pop to the bank, and then fly halfway around the world to create an improvised dam to hold back a raging torrent and save a village. But there are a few important provisos:

[1] Eat a good breakfast. Superheroes who skip breakfast report that they feel less able to concentrate, less able to perform amazing feats of strength, and generally feel less motivated.

[2] Always allow at least half an hour between eating and crime-fighting assignments, especially if they involve flying, climbing, or swimming.

[3] Drink lots of water and don't eat on the move.

By now you'll be well settled into your superhero routine, but things will be getting kind of hectic. You'll be juggling work and home life, breaking dates, letting your friends down, and generally feeling conflicted and confused. The next chapter shows you how to keep all the balls in the air, from making excuses to your partner, to keeping your fatal flaw a secret, and what to expect when you are lured to the dark side.

CHAPTER FIVE

CHAPTER SIX
Some Rain Must Fall

How to Find Your Evil Nemesis—
Even in a Crowded Shopping Mall

Your Fatal Flaw and How to Keep It a Secret

Twenty Excuses for Breaking a Date

The Lure of the Dark Side:
Deciding How to Use Your Powers

Never Forget You're Human
(Even If You're Not)

How to Find Your Evil Nemesis— Even in a Crowded Shopping Mall

Finding "the one"—that special person who is willing to dedicate their life to ending yours; who watches you while you sleep then jumps through the skylight with a chainsaw; the tall dark stranger who enjoys watching a sunset with you before trying to destroy civilization as you know it—isn't easy.

If you have met someone whose capacity for causing ruin, injury, and pain perfectly complements your own moral excellence, then congratulations. If you are still searching, don't despair. A deliverer of retributive vengeance can appear when you are least expecting it. But you won't find that person by sitting at home in front of an old movie inhaling a gallon of Rocky Road. The real question is, how do you meet someone that you'll really hate?

Five Rules of Hating

[1] Never try to kill your enemy on the first meeting.

[2] If you really don't get along, there is no obligation on either of you to commit to a lifelong vendetta. Let the relationship degenerate slowly and see where it leads.

[3] Try speed hating. It allows you to meet lots of potential enemies in one evening, and even if no one invites you back to their island dungeon, at least you'll have traded insults rather than stay home alone.

[4] Don't dismiss someone just because they aren't unpleasant or scheming enough. They may already have planted a pound of C4 underneath your chair.

[5] Don't set your standards too low. Not everyone can pair up with a scumbag alien life form with ambitions to rule the universe.

Confident superhero 35, 6' 5", blond, deep blue eyes, in great shape, nonsmoker, seeks bald, materialistic, facially disfigured whacko for evenings of mutual enmity. Inflexibility and loud maniacal laugh essential. Must have own rotary saw.

Merciless and emotionally insecure sociopath 47, 5' 4", bald, dark glasses, animal lover, Capricorn, seeks caped crusader to share sterile subterranean bunker. Animosity first, then candlelit torture, swims in shark pool, and eternal conflict. No strings—only chains and leather straps.

CHAPTER SIX

Conversation Starters

When meeting someone for the first time, there's nothing more embarrassing than that awkward silence after you've been introduced.

Here are ten ways to start up a volatile conversation:

[1] "Moonlight becomes you—total darkness even more."

[2] "Don't you love nature, despite what it did to you?"

[3] "Do you need a license to be that ugly?"

[4] "The inbreeding is certainly obvious in your family."

[5] "The next time you shave, why don't you stand a little closer to the razor?"

[6] "Aren't you depriving a village somewhere of an idiot?"

[7] "How much does a polar bear weigh? Enough to break the ice." (Guaranteed to cause an awkward silence.)

[8] "Were you the first in your family born without a tail?"

[9] "Whatever kind of look you were going for, you missed."

[10] "You look much shorter in person."

Body Language: How to Tell if Someone Wants to Kill You

Everyone gives away their thoughts with subtle body clues. Your nemesis may appear perfectly charming, but their body language will reveal how they really feel about you. They may want to kill you if they:

[1] turn their body away, avoid eye contact, and whisper something to a large bald man wearing a suit.

[2] slip something into your drink.

[3] bang their fist down on the table and say "enough."

[4] bite their lip so hard that they draw blood.

[5] appear preoccupied with a small black box containing a large red button.

[6] grin menacingly while stroking a long-haired white cat.

[7] square up to you, nose to nose, and talk rapidly in a low insistent voice.

[8] spit in your face.

[9] use phrases like "It has been nice knowing you" or "I am going to enjoy watching you die."

If your nemesis-to-be appears to drop off the planet after what seemed to be a perfect initial confrontation, don't despair. They may be at home planning ways to end your life. As for spotting your potential nemesis in a crowded shopping mall: archvillains are masters of subterfuge and disguise, so your guess is as good as ours.

Your Fatal Flaw and How to Keep It a Secret

Every superhero needs a fatal flaw to raise the stakes in a conflict and to give their enemies a sporting chance. An invincible superhero is dull and predictable. Having a fatal flaw makes you more interesting, more human. But that doesn't mean you should brag about it down at the bar.

The most famous flaw in the world belonged to Achilles, and it was, of course, his Achilles-heel. Now, there's a lesson right there. When you actually get a flaw named after you, you know you've screwed up big time. In his favor, he didn't actually know that the back of his foot was going to bail, so he can't be accused of either flaunting it or being negligent in his choice of footwear.

If you know what your flaw is, then naturally it is wise to keep it secret and well protected. For instance, when you apply for that cruddy job as a pizza delivery boy, and the guy in the interview asks, "What's your biggest weakness?" don't mention the flaw. Although it is advisable to carry a fatal flaw medical card or a discrete Medic Alert bracelet, because if you end up unconscious in the hospital the medics will want to know what's wrong with you and may overlook the obvious (e.g., a silver bullet lodged in your windpipe).

Sometimes protecting a flaw can draw attention to the very thing that you are trying to hide. Use reverse psychology instead. For instance, if you have a weak chin, don't walk around with your head down in a lame attempt to protect it. Do the opposite. Flaunt it. Grow a beard. And not

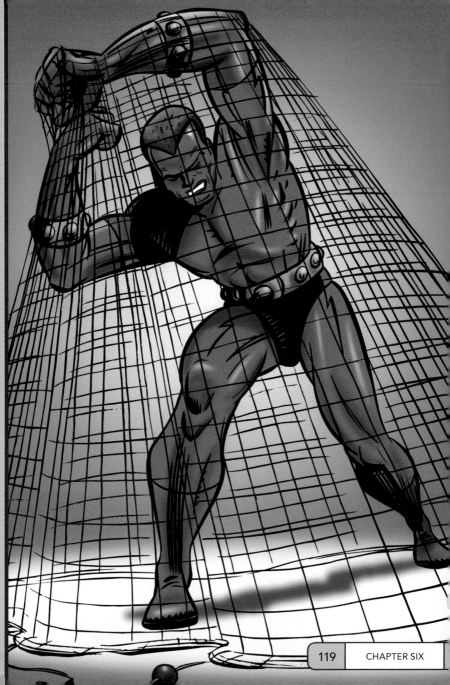

one of those scraggly Beatnik chin bushes, but an awesome biblical beard—a huge shaggy Founding Father mane that announces to the world that you are more intelligent and sexually potent than your beardless contemporaries. Show an exaggerated interest in other people's chins. They'll never suspect the truth.

In "The Birthmark" the great nineteenth-century writer Nathaniel Hawthorne tells the story of a scientist who is married to an impossibly beautiful woman who has but one shortcoming: a birthmark on her face that repels him. He applies his vast intellect and scientific knowledge to remove this solitary imperfection. He succeeds, but kills her in the process. So take a lesson from this little apologue: embrace your imperfections, be always mindful of the conflict between the human condition and scientific knowledge, and stay away from plastic surgeons.

Twenty Excuses for Breaking a Date

Breaking dates is a crime-fighting occupational hazard. Whether you're a cop or a caped crusader, fulfilling your amorous commitments is a major challenge. Here are some excuses to choose from the next time you have to blow someone off.

[1] I've had a tough time at work. I've been climbing the walls all day.

[2] Something's come up at work. It's potentially an explosive situation; I need to stay late and try to defuse it.

[3] I have a train to catch.

[4] I have to recharge my batteries.

[5] I'm having laser treatment; I don't know if I can get away.

[6] I promised to help a friend iron his collection of capes.

[7] Sorry, I've been on a short fuse recently.

[8] I'm waiting for an old colleague to fly in.

[9] I'm on a macro-bionic diet.

[10] If you must know, I'm feeling a bit drawn.

[11] My work here is nearly done. I'll call you when I've finished.

[12] I really am tied up right now.

[13] I've got something in my eye. I'll call you as soon as my other senses have compensated.

[14] I'm trapped in a small dinghy off the coast of Uruguay.

[15] I've got to stay home and practice my alliteration.

[16] I have to run a few errands.

[17] My plane got held up.

[18] Something big is about to blow. Can I ring you back in 23 seconds?

[19] I've lost my glasses.

[20] I'm expecting an important phone call.

The Lure of the Dark Side: Deciding How to Use Your Powers

Being tempted by the attractions of the dark side will be a recurrent theme during your career. Being head-hunted by the forces of evil can be very flattering, but it leaves you with a difficult choice. Not because there's any great moral decision to make. The real questions are these: Are the overall package and fringe benefits of the dark side better than those you currently enjoy? Is the grass greener, and more importantly, does it stay greener? In other words—can you get away with it?

The greatest stories are myths about the struggle between good and evil, and they all drum home the message that good triumphs in the end. That's powerful conditioning to stay away from the naughty stuff. The evil ones are portrayed over and over as unfulfilled, dissatisfied, and disillusioned with their destiny, either trapped in a cycle of evil-doing while secretly wishing to reform, or way beyond redemption. But is it true?

How can you make a decision if you don't know about the dark side? Would you go on holiday without seeing a brochure? Would you buy a car without test-driving it first? Why should you join any organization that hides in the shadows and markets itself so abysmally? Here is a checklist of questions you should ask anyone who invites you to join his ruinous cabal, even if he claims to be your father:

What's in it for me?
Always make sure you know what you're going to get out of it. Don't accept vague promises like "together we could rule the universe."

Is there a cooling-off period? Before entering into any Faustian pact, make sure there is a twenty-eight-day cooling off period, so if you are dissatisfied, you can return to do-gooding and no regrets. This allows time to evaluate a decision made in haste or under pressure. Public confidence in the dark side has always been damaged by the prevailing perception that there's no turning back. Also, don't be pressured by the "join me today, or the deal is off" hard sell. The dark side will still be there tomorrow, so don't be rushed into a making a decision today.

What's the average IQ?

There's an old adage about a guy that was shown heaven and hell. In heaven there were lots of people enjoying a sumptuous banquet with eight-foot chopsticks. Since the chopsticks were too long for one person to use, they all fed each other. Then the man visited hell, where he saw the same banquet, same chopsticks, but everyone was miserable and hungry, ostensibly because they were too selfish to feed each other, or too stupid to use their hands.

Can I see some testimonials?

Ask to see testimonials from others who have joined the dark side, or better still, speak to them in person.

What clothes should I pack?

Evil has always been associated with extremes of temperature, from the burning fires of hell to the freezing wastelands of exile. There is nothing worse than turning up on your first day at the dark side dressed in sealskins and furry boots, to find that everyone else is wearing a thong and flip-flops. Or else, you dress up all gothic and they are Abercrombie & Fitch™. Check the prevailing conditions and fashions before you pack, and always ensure that there is adequate air-conditioning.

CHAPTER SIX

Never Forget You're Human (Even If You're Not)

Now that you have worked out who you are, have focused your powers, told your parents, found a place of your own, honed your skills, and ideally, have committed to fight for all that is good and true, it is absolutely imperative that you keep your identity a secret.

After all that you have been through, it would be a real waste to blow it now. So, apart from adopting a flimsy disguise, how do you stop the world from invading your privacy and exposing you as a caped crusader?

If in doubt, return to what you know best—being a geek. Humans expect humility, either on your part or theirs. So never forget you're human—even if you're not, keep your true identity a secret, drink plenty of fluids, and always use the handrail when boarding or exiting from a bus. And most important of all: Every wretched hive of scum and villainy is someone's home town.

The next chapter helps you to come to terms with the twilight years of crime fighting. It shows how to tell when it's time to hang up the cape, and how to merchandise your own image and explore new career opportunities.

CHAPTER SEVEN
The Vegas Years

How to Reinvent Yourself
How to Merchandise Your Own Image
To Heroism and Beyond
Signs It's Time to Hang Up Your Cape

How to Reinvent Yourself

If you want to be a superhero with staying power you must be prepared to reinvent yourself over and over again. This means taking a good hard look at your image and value system and thinking up ways to appeal to the latest generation that don't involve wearing inappropriate capes, having Botox injections, or buying a sportier supermobile.

Why, you may ask, if you ain't broke, should you fix yourself? Why reinvent the wheel? If so, you clearly consider yourself part of a transcendental value system and you mistakenly see yourself as an immutable symbol of right, might, and the correct way. Or maybe you really believe you are a small disc revolving on an axel to facilitate motion. Whatever your self-image issues, you haven't been reading your Nietzsche.

Superheroes are constantly discovering and rediscovering themselves. They create their own good and evil based on what helps them to succeed and realize their potential. If their motivations produce results that the majority of the population find acceptable, they are known as "goodies"; if their desires are harmful to the majority they are called "baddies".

For Nietzsche, everything in the world, including morality, is transitory and is being continually reinvented. A superhero should take comfort from this and actually embrace change.

Stand in front of the mirror and do this now. Look at your body. Turn sideways and appreciate your profile. Feels good doesn't it? You are something you've always admired about yourself, but don't be fooled into thinking you own a freehold for the moral high ground. How many times for you have the ends justified the means? How often have you made dubious moral decisions to pursue what you consider the greatest good? A superhero should master the practice of overcoming themselves, while at the same time being accessible to a new wave of superhero worshippers.

The best way to appeal to the younger generation is to tell them all about your earliest origins. This is counterintuitive, since in normal circumstances, anyone over fifty doing a big nostalgic flashback to when they were a kid, or what they did at school, or who they kissed at the prom, would be a big yawn, but at the moment the public just can't seem to get enough of superhero prequels. So if you want to be a media-savvy super with a future, keep changing but don't stop looking back—it's the new forward.

How to Merchandise Your Own Image

Years after retirement, many superheroes are able to generate considerable interest and financial rewards by exploiting their merchandising appeal.

Children and certain adults love to play with action figures, and collect memorabilia associated with them. Licensed products make up over one-third of the toy industry, and the market share just keeps on growing. Superhero spin-offs and products are dominant players in this area, and a canny silver-haired super can get a piece of this action and cash in on a big earner. Learning to fly was easy; knowing how to fly off store shelves is a bigger challenge.

First, when you are choosing your "look"—your costume, accessories, even your side-kick—it is important that you consider how these elements will respond to miniaturisation and reproduction in action figure form. If elements of your outfit are too elaborate, they will have to be simplified to keep the unit cost down and you'll be left with a shoddy representation that won't do you justice. So before you make any image choices, ask yourself how they will look in flesh-colored vinyl with fully-articulating limbs gripped tightly within a chubby adolescent fist.

Second, you've got to associate yourself with a large reproducible object, so that whoever buys your action figure will feel compelled to have the shark tank, siege tower, supermobile, or secret lair that is an inseparable part of your identity. If you live on an island or an elaborate space station you've hit the jackpot: that's five pounds of plastic and six months worth of pocket money right there.

Third, don't limit yourself to one arch-enemy and deprive your loyal fan base of the thrill of collecting a stable of costly villains.

Above all you've got to be keyed into the compelling lifestyle choices that you represent. What is it about you (and them) which makes them want to be you? How do you tap into their wants, needs, and desires? How do you achieve that delicate balance of ensuring that supply is woefully insufficient to meet demand?

Don't give them what they don't really want, and they'll be lining up around the block to have what they can't get.

135 | CHAPTER SEVEN

To Heroism and Beyond

Decades ago, when life was shorter and work was more physically demanding, retirement was more about recovery than living. But today, even a retirement can be lived in the fast lane, and we are all living longer too. Life after crime fighting is nearly another lifetime. So, before you think of trading in your supermobile for a golf cart, consider these active alternatives.

Stunt Work

This is a good choice for a retired super because it makes full use of physical skills, courage, and love of action. Some supers have special qualities that will ensure that they are never out of work (e.g., body duplication, bursting into flames, martial arts). However all you really need is a large collection of lumberjack shirts, a pick-up truck, and an ability to tolerate a single topic of conversation: how many bones you've broken. Even though you are indestructible, you'll soon get the hang of the banter, which goes something like: "Yeah, I got knocked out cold six times last month . . . I was hospitalized with a cracked sternum . . . it was touch and go there . . . the docs had to rebuild my shoulder for the fifth time this year, etc. . . . ."

If you're the stunt double for a big Hollywood player, they're the star, not you, which can give your ego a bruising if you're used to being the center of attention. Now you know what your sidekick had to put up with all those years. It's a humbling experience, but driving an earthmover through a wall of flame is better than collecting carts at the supermarket.

Write your own fanfic

Enact all the fantasies that you never had a chance to realize from the comfort of your own PC. There's nothing more thrilling than being part of a worldwide community of adoring fans. It won't pay the bills, but it will allow you to meet a bunch of people who still think you're rather special.

Sell kitchen appliances

Supers and professional boxers have a lot in common, besides their punching power: whatever other careers you try, a part of you is always waiting for the comeback. At some point in the future you may indeed be called up for one final assignment, but you can't build a retirement on what if.

Selling kitchen grills is another matter. People rely on celebrities to tell them how to cook their meat products and are willing to pay top dollar for an endorsement.

Motivational speaking

Become a leading authority on the development of human potential and personal effectiveness. Pass on your

burning message of reality-based motivation and get a big fat check for your trouble plus all your incidental costs paid for by gullible business clients.

Clearly, you can't actually teach ordinary folk how to see through walls or bend metal bars, but that shouldn't stop you from giving on-site management training and keynote presentations with titles like "Using Your Fists as a Catalyst for Change" and "Throwing Buildings and Shaking Up the Workplace."

If you don't feel comfortable talking in public, just perform an impressive feat of strength and flex your muscles. As long as you give a brief demonstration of your skills, delegates will be convinced that they can apply the same principles to their business or personal life. Even a brief roar executed with sufficient menace will be interpreted as a refreshingly straightforward business guru statement and the CEOs will feel they have progressed a little further in their quest for an enlightened corporate culture.

Mentoring

Those who can't do, teach, but those who could, mentor. There will always be a moment during the training of your young ward where you will be required to show that you still possess your formidable powers. You will, in true mentor style, be obliged to utter the timeworn mentor dictum "I don't want any trouble," followed by a ferocious demonstration of physicality resulting in the public humiliation of someone who has been bullying your student and mistakes you for an easy target.

Choreography

You've got the tights, the stamina, and all the moves, so why not become a choreographer? Next to joining the army, it is the only way to push people way beyond the limits of physical exhaustion without actually breaking the law.

Signs It's Time to Hang Up Your Cape

Retirement is not something that springs on you. It creeps up slowly. Here are a few warning signs that it's time to hang up your cape:

[1] You've traded in your supermobile for a golf cart.

[2] Your favorite gadget is your electric toothbrush.

[3] You begin every other sentence with, "Nowadays . . . "

[4] You don't fight crime after 7:30 in the evening.

[5] Your new easy chair has more options than your supermobile.

[6] Your sidekick is dating someone half their age, and isn't breaking any laws.

[7] The candles on your birthday cake generate more heat than your thermo vision.

[8] You enjoy cutting coupons more than the crime rate.

[9] Whenever you hit the streets you take an umbrella and a sweater.

[10] You used to stick to walls—now you're glued to the television.

CHAPTER SEVEN

Epilogue

We wish you a long and prosperous career, whichever galaxy it takes you to. Whatever happens, never stop telling yourself how special you are, because if you don't believe in super you, who else will?

Now get out there and start soaring over the cityscape in search of the scourges of society. The eternal conflict between good and evil will never end, so what are you waiting for . . .

CHAPTER SEVEN

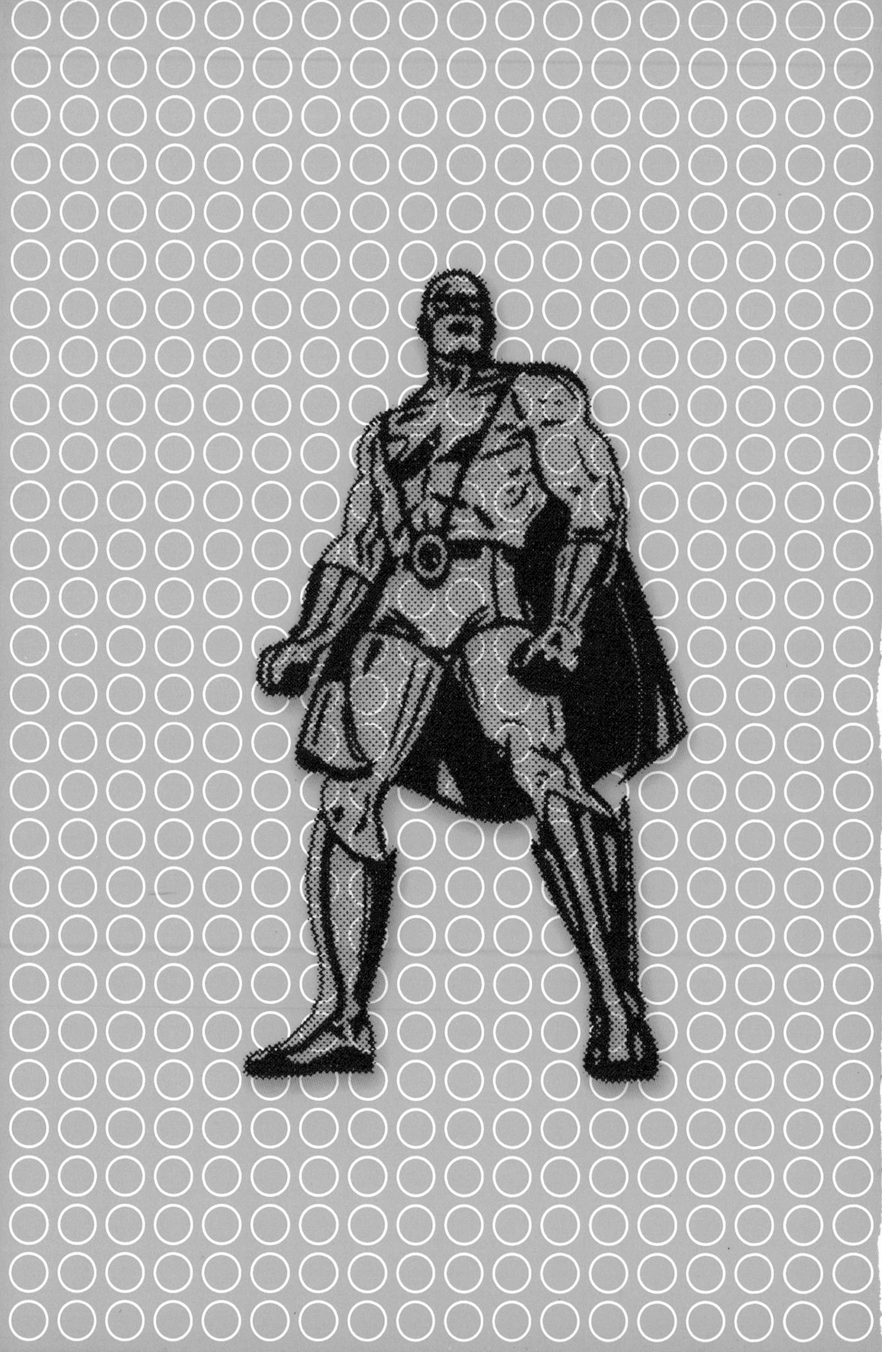